INDEPENDENT BUSES OF YORKSHIRE

JOHN LAW

AMBERLEY

The Doncaster area was once famous for its independent bus companies, particularly to the east of the town. Blue Canoe once served the Doncaster to Armthorpe route using a 1926-built Reo Pullman twenty-seat bus registered WU 5893. Blue Canoe, in business since 1921, later became part of the small Blue Line/Reliance Empire until takeover by South Yorkshire PTE in 1979.

First published 2020

Amberley Publishing
The Hill, Stroud
Gloucestershire, GL5 4EP

www.amberley-books.com

Copyright © John Law, 2020

The right of John Law to be identified as
the Author of this work has been asserted in
accordance with the Copyrights, Designs and
Patents Act 1988.

ISBN 978 1 4456 9561 7 (print)
ISBN 978 1 4456 9562 4 (ebook)

British Library Cataloguing in Publication Data.
A catalogue record for this book is available from
the British Library.

Typesetting by Aura Technology and Software
Services, India. Printed in the UK.

Introduction

The vast county of Yorkshire, from the splendour of the Dales and the North York Moors to the industrial landscapes of the Don Valley and South Teesside, is a land of great contrasts.

At this point it is appropriate to define the extent of Yorkshire for the purposes of this book. Until the 1974 boundary changes, Yorkshire consisted of three Ridings: East, North and West. Our wonderful politicians saw the creation of Humberside and Cleveland (these have since been abolished) and, even worse, the loss of parts of the area to the west of Skipton to the traditional 'enemy' – Lancashire! To make things clear, this publication covers the whole of what was, traditionally, Yorkshire.

The author was both born and brought up in Yorkshire, having arrived into this world in Middlesbrough in 1951 and was educated in the opposite end of the county, at Doncaster. He developed an interest in public road transport during the mid-1960s and fondly remembers the colourful variety of independent bus companies to be found in the town.

Indeed, Doncaster was a fantastic place to find the smaller operators of the area. The Blue Line/Reliance partnership, along with Felix Motors and Premier, ran services eastwards from a terminus at Christchurch, Doncaster, to the large mining communities to the east. Blue Line extended its reach through the flatlands to Goole.

Other Doncaster independents included Leon of Finningley and a trio of small companies operating out to Rossington, a large mining village.

The rest of what is now South Yorkshire also provided rich pickings for bus enthusiasts. Wigmore's and Booth & Fisher served Sheffield, while Barnsley had a small host of independents, the last of which was Larratt Pepper of Thurnscoe.

The city of Wakefield, once the capital of the West Riding, was, until 1967, the centre of operations of Britain's largest independent bus company – the West Riding Automobile Company. Another large business not in any major group was Wallace Arnold, with stage carriage services in Leeds and Scarborough.

The area now known as West Yorkshire was once home to another big independent, Ledgards, who had a fantastically interesting fleet. One of the last names to disappear was South Yorkshire Road Transport. Despite its name, it was based in Pontefract, West Yorkshire. That area also saw United Services and Ford's of Ackworth, while Dewsbury and Mirfield had Woods and Longstaff's serving them.

The eastern side of Yorkshire only had a few independents, with Connor & Graham in Hull and Primrose Valley in Filey.

Further inland is the centre of the known universe, the city of York. Here York Pullman, Reliance, Majestic and several smaller concerns could be found. Beyond there, in the old North Riding, was the territory of BTC-owned United, with only a few small companies breaking the monopoly, Saltburn Motor Services being one of them.

However, in 1986, with Margaret Thatcher in power, deregulation came. Literally hundreds of small bus companies throughout Yorkshire took to the roads, some running competitive routes, while others gained tendered services from local councils. Inevitably, many of these fell by the wayside, either victims of takeovers, competition or economic circumstances. The same fate occurred to a good number of the established operators. Nevertheless, places like Middlesbrough, Sheffield and Hull were attracting enthusiasts wanting to photograph, or just experience, the ever-changing scene.

Today's independent bus scene is still interesting and a trip to 'God's Own Country' can be thoroughly recommended. Why not try some fish and chips or a decent drop of Yorkshire beer while you are here?

With such a vast subject to cover in less than 100 pages, it is inevitable that some bus companies have been omitted. It would have been nice to have included a few more vehicles from each operator as well. Apologies are due if your favourite vehicle or firm is not included. Maybe there is scope for second volume?

Finally, thanks are due to the following for providing photographs and information: Bus Lists on the Web, the late Les Flint, Keith Jenkinson, Jim Sambrooks, Peter Tuffrey and Andrew Warnes.

In the early part of the twenty-first century, Abbey Coaches were to be found operating a local service in the small North Yorkshire town of Guisborough. Seen on Westgate in July 2005 is ex-Northern General twenty-five-seat Optare Metrorider M936 FTN. Abbey Coaches are no longer trading.

The 1980s saw Huddersfield-based coach company Abbeyways enter the stage carriage market with services around the area. Seen in Huddersfield bus station, prior to setting out on a journey to Leeds in spring 1988, is PHG 777P. Still in the colours of its previous operator, Hyndburn Transport, this Leyland Atlantean AN68/1R has seventy-eight-seat bodywork by East Lancs. Abbeyways also took over Woods of Mirfield and a further vehicle is shown on page 92 from that era.

Acklams is a small operator from the fine East Yorkshire town of Beverley. As well as private hire and coaching, the company runs several local bus routes, including the Beverley town service. Engaged on such a duty, on 19 August 2010, is thirty-two-seat Optare Solo SR YX10 AAU.

The years after deregulation saw the introduction of minibuses into the competitive world of bus operation, including the independent sector. AJC Coaches, also trading as Angloblue, had a depot near Elland Road football stadium in Leeds. From there they operated a few local routes around the city. In February 1994, G314 CKB, a Mercedes 609D twenty-four-seat vehicle, is seen in central Leeds passing the Corn Exchange on a service to Beeston. The company has since ceased trading.

Aldham Coaches was one of several operators to take advantage of deregulation in the area around Barnsley. Although in later years more conventional buses were used on stage carriage work, Leyland Leopard coaches were the mainstay of operations. In 1986, CHA 457K is seen against a backdrop of brutalist architecture near Barnsley Market. This Plaxton-bodied coach had been new to Midland Red as fleet No. 6457. Like many of the independents in the area, stage carriage work is no longer undertaken.

Alpha Bus and Coach was awarded the contract to operate three 'Park & Ride' services in Hull. On one such duty is YX03 MWJ, a forty-one-seat Dennis Dart SLF/Plaxton combination. It is seen on Anlaby Road, close to Hull city centre, on 11 July 2006. Alpha was soon to be taken over by Dunn-Line, who sold out to Veolia. East Yorkshire Motor Services later purchased the Hull operation.

Amberley Travel appeared on the streets of Leeds after deregulation, operating route 88/X88 to Pudsey. The service was later taken over by Black Prince, a larger independent. Seen arriving into the Central bus station in Leeds in early 1988 is Leyland National KCG 608L. This vehicle had been new as a forty-nine-seat bus with Alder Valley.

Andrews was a Sheffield-based operator that had, prior to deregulation, been a PSV driver-training organisation. A variety of double-deck buses were used on the stage carriage services. An example is former West Midlands PTE SDA 694S (named *Maid Marion*), a Leyland Fleetline bodied by MCW. It is seen loading up on Paternoster Row in central Sheffield in the summer of 1990. Andrews was later taken over by the Yorkshire Traction Group.

Applebys was a company that originally operated from a depot at Conisholme in Lincolnshire, which expanded into East Yorkshire after the takeover of Boddys of Bridlington. As well as a competitive open-top service in Scarborough, stage carriage operations were undertaken, such as a route from Bridlington to Flamborough. It's on such a duty that we see FRH 615T, a Bedford YMT/Plaxton coach, new to Boddys in 1979, in the village of Flamborough in 1987. Applebys has since ceased trading.

Aston Express was one of those businesses that started stage carriage service after the introduction of deregulation. A variety of vehicles was owned, running a few routes around the Sheffield area. One of the locations served was the small shopping centre at Crystal Peaks, where R567 UOT was photographed in late 1997. This forty-seat Dennis Dart SLF/UVG had been bought new earlier in the year. Aston Express lost its licences to operate bus services in 2004.

The small West Yorkshire town of Holmfirth is best known as the home of the long–running BBC comedy *Last of the Summer Wine*. It was also where bus operator Baddeley Brothers had their base, running various services in the area, with Holmfirth to Penistone being the most frequent route. On such a duty, high above Dunford Bridge in 1975, is fleet No. 87 (RJX 253). This little Weymann-bodied Albion Nimbus had been new to Halifax Corporation in 1962. Baddeley Brothers was taken over by West Yorkshire PTE in 1976.

Beeston's was one of those small companies that began services in the Middlesbrough area after deregulation. Operating a local route and seen entering the town's bus station in spring 1988 is SAO 900N, a Duple-bodied Bedford YRQ coach. This had been new to Mandale of Greystoke, Cumbria.

Bigfoot Buses was the name given to the first stage carriage operations of Geldard's Coaches of Leeds. They ran between 1995 and 1998. Seen in autumn 1997 is Leyland National PJI 3670, leaving Vicar Lane in Leeds to join the Headrow. Details of this vehicle's history have proved unobtainable, but it is believed that it started life with Hants & Dorset.

Another post-deregulation operator in West Yorkshire, BL Travel, has a base at Kinsley and runs frequent services into Wakefield and Pontefract. A blue livery is normally applied to service buses, as seen on V453 NGA in Wakefield on 6 February 2010. This Wright-bodied Volvo B6BLE had been new to Whitelaw of Stonehouse, Scotland.

Black Prince started out as a minibus operator in 1969 and progressed into stage carriage operation following deregulation. The company's main operating area centred on Leeds and Morley. Seen in City Square, Leeds, in June 2004 is 704 (F704 JCN), an Alexander-bodied Scania N111DRB. This bus had been new to Kentish Bus.

Black Prince liked the Volvo Ailsa/Alexander and had plenty of them. However, a more unusual vehicle in the fleet was 380 (LWB 380P), an Ailsa B55-10 with Irish-built Van Hool McArdle bodywork. This was one of many that were purchased by South Yorkshire PTE. It was photographed on a private hire duty at Westwoodside, getting close to its destination of the Sandtoft trolleybus museum in July 1991. Sadly, Black Prince sold out to Yorkshire Rider/First Group in 2005.

In the mid-1990s Blue Bus, a Manchester-based operator, opened a depot in Huddersfield and began stage carriage services in that area. Seen at the Yorkshire town's bus station in mid-1996 is fleet No. 1 (K1 BLU). This forty-seat Dennis Dart, with East Lancs bodywork, had been new to the company in 1993. The Yorkshire operations ceased just after this photograph was taken.

Alphabetically the first of the Doncaster independents to feature in these pages, Blue Ensign (GH Ennifer) began operating a service to Rossington in 1920. Over the years a great variety of buses had been owned. One of great interest was FDT 202, a 1948-built Crossley DD42/5. Scottish Aviation built the fifty-six-seat body. The location is the old Glasgow Paddocks bus station in Doncaster, c. 1960. Blue Ensign was sold to South Yorkshire PTE in 1978.

Blue Line (S Morgan), based at Armthorpe, ran services out of Doncaster in association with Reliance (R Store) of Stainforth. Seen at its Christchurch terminus in Doncaster, *c.* 1961, is FPT 205. This Guy Arab II had been delivered to Sunderland District in 1943 and received a new Roe body in 1953. It had been bought by Blue Line in 1961 and lasted until 1967.

Blue Line certainly liked their Guy Arabs! The last one was bought in 1967 and is seen here on 1 February 1968, arriving at its Doncaster destination. This Guy Arab V, registered RWY 891F, had a seventy-three-seat Roe body. When Blue Line was sold to South Yorkshire PTE in March 1979, this vehicle was included in the sale but was never used. (Les Flint)

Based at the village of Halfway, South Yorkshire, Booth & Fisher operated several routes in the area between Sheffield and Worksop. The company favoured Albion Nimbus types for its more rural services. This 1959-built example, with thirty-one-seat Willowbrook bodywork, had originally been a demonstrator. 537 JTC is seen at the depot in 1977. Strictly speaking, this is in South Yorkshire PTE days, as the company had been purchased in 1975, but remained a separate enterprise for several years.

Brecks International was a small coach company in Rotherham. In late 1989, when this photo was taken, a bus service from Sheffield to Dinnington was being operated. Seen at Pond Street bus station in Sheffield is PHL 454R, a rare Bristol LHS6L with thirty-five-seat Plaxton coachwork. It had been new to the business in 1977. Brecks' venture into stage carriage work did not last long.

Wombwell-based operator T. Burrows & Sons sold out to Yorkshire Traction in October 1966, though none of the rather varied fleet was used by the larger company. Services ran as far as Barnsley, Wakefield and Leeds. A dark red livery was employed, as seen (albeit in monochrome) on No. 91 (SWU 914). This AEC Reliance/Burlingham forty-five-seat saloon had been new to the company in 1956. It is seen in the depot, _c._ 1960.

Burrows of Wombwell No. 97 (9491 WY), a Bedford SB1 with Yeates coachwork, featuring forty-four bus seats, is seen outside the depot on the same occasion as the upper photograph.

In the 1970s, Cherry Coaches ran a town service in Beverley, deep in the heart of East Yorkshire territory. On a dark winter day *c.* 1975, YAL 368 is seen loading up in the town's small bus station. This Leyland Tiger Cub with forty-four-seat Metro-Cammell bodywork had been new to East Midland, numbered R368, in 1958.

Cherry Coaches later bought lightweight vehicles (apart from double-deckers used on school runs). NWL 652M, a former City of Oxford Ford R1014/Willowbrook saloon, was a regular performer on the town service. Alongside, at the depot, is Ford R1114/Duple coach DNU 14T. It had originally been delivered to a Derbyshire operator. Cherry Coaches sold out to East Yorkshire Motor Services in 1987, with the former owner, Mr 'Bob' Cherry, passing away in 2011, aged eighty-eight.

City Central was one of those independents that sprang up in the years following deregulation in the Hull area. Seen outside Paragon railway station in the summer of 2001 is 219 (KKU 111W), a former South Yorkshire PTE Dennis Dominator bodied by Alexander.

City Central also brought back the old Kingston upon Hull Corporation Transport colour scheme, as illustrated on 237 (PAZ 5360). Originally registered SUA 149R, this Roe-bodied Leyland Atlantean AN68A/1R had been new to West Yorkshire PTE. Again, it is seen alongside Hull Paragon station in summer 2001. The company's bus operation has since ceased.

Clarksons Coaches was a small operator based in South Elmsall in West Yorkshire. Around the beginning of the twenty-first century, bus services were being run towards Wakefield and Barnsley. It is at the latter location that we see V676 FPO in spring 2001. This Dennis Dart SLF/ Caetano bus had been new two years earlier to a Birkenhead company. The Clarkson family sold the business in 2008 and it ceased trading in 2011.

Coachcraft was a converter of panel vans based in Doncaster. In the early years of deregulation, it commenced stage carriage operations in the town. About to depart for Armthorpe from its Christchurch terminus in early 1987 is URF 725L. New to Chase Coaches of Staffordshire, it is a Ford R1014 with Duple Dominant forty-five-seat coach body. Coachcraft's venture into bus operation did not last long. (Jim Sambrooks)

Connexions Buses, also known as Harrogate Coach Travel, have sizeable operations in the North and West Yorkshire area. Harrogate Coach Travel was the original name adopted for the bus fleet, back in the 1980s, and Scania Omnicity saloon 9936 UB was repainted into those colours when photographed in Harrogate on 10 January 2019. Originally registered YN05 HZY, it had been new to Manchester operator Bullock of Cheadle.

Connexions Buses-owned thirty-seat Optare Solo SR YJ65 EVH was found on a sunny 4 May 2017 on a local service passing the railway station in York. This bus had been new to the company in 2015. At the time of writing, late 2019, there were five Solos in the fleet.

Connor & Graham, based at Easington in the Holderness flatlands to the east of Hull, ran into that city on a regular basis. Seen at its westerly terminus on 22 June 1962 is ASD 706. This 1945-built 'utility' Guy Arab II/Northern Counties was photographed by the Late Les Flint, still in the colours of Western SMT, its original operator.

At the same spot, in 1988, is Connor & Graham's XJA 508L, a former Greater Manchester Leyland Atlantean AN68/1R with bodywork by Park Royal. Connor & Graham sold their stage carriage operations to East Yorkshire in 1993.

One of many companies to take advantage of deregulation in South Yorkshire, Cygnet Travel operated out of a depot in Darton, with services running into nearby Wakefield and Barnsley. Seen in the modernised bus station in the latter town is VRC 612Y, photographed in autumn 1996. Fourteen years earlier this Leyland Leopard/Plaxton Supreme Express fifty-three-seat coach had been new to Barton Transport of Nottinghamshire. After this photograph was taken the vehicle was painted into full Cygnet Travel livery and later went into preservation. Sadly, it was severely damaged in the fire at the Nottingham Heritage Centre at Ruddington.

Procter's of Leeming Bar today operate services in North Yorkshire using the trading name of Dales & District. For these operations a fleet of Optare Solos is utilised, supplemented by larger buses such as KJZ 13. Originally registered as NX59 BYC, this Volvo B7RLE/Wright B42F had been new to associated company Compass Royston of Stockton. It is seen in Northallerton on 25 April 2018 on the frequent service 73 to Bedale.

The Phillipson family, trading as Dearneways, commenced the operation of buses in 1949, transporting miners around the small South Yorkshire town of Goldthorpe. It was not until 1964 that a license was obtained for a limited stop bus operation between Thurnscoe and Sheffield, via Goldthorpe, Wath-on-Dearne and Rotherham. Seen at its Sheffield terminus, Pond Street bus station in early 1981, is AWJ 293T. This Leyland Leopard/Plaxton Supreme Express fifty-one-seat coach turned out to be the last vehicle delivered new to Dearneways, as the company sold out to South Yorkshire PTE in October 1981.

Don Motors was a small bus company with a share of the lucrative Doncaster to Rossington service. The entire fleet is seen in this view close to the depot on the former Great North Road in Bessacarr, *c.* 1960. Closest to the camera is EDT 680, an all-Leyland PD1A bought new in 1947. In the middle is ex-Maidstone & District Bristol K6A HKR 41. At the rear is VDT 94, a Burlingham-bodied Leyland PD2/20 new to Don Motors in 1956 and the only bus to be retained by East Midland Motor Services after the takeover in 1962.

K&H Doyle Coaches began operating buses from a base in Ripley, Derbyshire, in 1986, mainly on council tendered services, with a few commercial routes. At one stage, the Yorkshire city of Sheffield was also served, and it is in the Interchange there that we see N996 KUS on 19 April 2008. This Mercedes 709D/Wadham Stringer combination had been new to a Preston operator in 1995. K&H Doyle Coaches ceased trading in 2014, citing cuts in council funding as the reason.

Another Middlesbrough operator to start services after deregulation was Escort Coaches. These did not last long, though the company is still trading. Photographed on a dull day in Middlesbrough bus station was PFS 563M, a former Eastern Scottish Leyland Leopard with Alexander Y type bodywork. (Jim Sambrooks)

Felix Motors of Hatfield served the area to the east of Doncaster and the company was well known for its use of Roe-bodied AEC Regent double-deckers. No apology is given for including two of them on this page. Here we have one of the earlier ones, No. 34 (OWX 283), a Regent III with fifty-eight seats, bought new in 1955. It is seen at Christchurch, Doncaster, on 5 June 1967. (Les Flint)

Felix No. 42 (8176 WY), a 1961-built AEC Regent V with Roe bodywork featuring seventy-three seats and rear platform doors, is seen departing from RAF Lindholme. This facility closed in 1982 and the site now holds a penal institution. Felix Motors succumbed to the might of South Yorkshire PTE in 1976, just after this photograph was taken. (Jim Sambrooks)

When Turton's of Ackworth ceased trading in the early 1960s, the bus service to the nearby town of Pontefract passed to another Ackworth operator Ford's Coaches. A regular performer on such duties was Leyland Leopard/Willowbrook fifty-three-seat saloon CYG 423H, bought new in 1970. It is seen departing Pontefract bus station in 1977. Larger independent South Yorkshire Road Transport took over in 1985.

Four Seasons was a post-deregulation operator that began running services out of Leeds, mainly in a south-easterly direction. However, this photograph was taken in Morley, south-west of the city, in early 1989, when banks still had branches in small towns. Three are visible behind GLS 273N, a former Midland Scottish Leyland Leopard with Alexander Y type bodywork. The stage carriage operations were sold to West Riding in 1993.

It is pleasing to note that Glenn Coaches of Wiggington (a suburb of York) are very much still in business, though the company no longer operates stage carriage routes. Like many businesses, advantage was taken of the freedoms given by deregulation and several local services were to be found in the city when this photograph was taken in the spring of 1990. Though, in later years, some second-hand Leyland Nationals were employed, 'heavyweight' coaches were the mainstay of bus operations. PSD 125R, a Leyland Leopard/Plaxton Supreme Express, had been new to Frazer of Fairlie for use in its Clyde Coast bus operations in Scotland. It is seen opposite the railway station in York.

Another Yorkshire coach company, Globe of Barnsley, tried its hand at bus service work. It operated mainly tendered operations and still does to this day. Seen at Barnsley Interchange in January 1992 is C803 KBT. This unusual vehicle is an Optare-bodied Leyland Cub that had been new as fleet number 1803 with West Yorkshire PTE.

Gorwood Brothers, based at East Cottingwith, a small East Riding village, ran a bus service into the city of York in the 1970s. A fleet of rather ancient, but smart, Bedford coaches was employed on such duties. This example, SED 232, a 1958-built SB3/Duple Vega forty-one-seater, is seen parked up near Layerthorpe in York, *c.* 1976.

Very much a product of deregulation, Groves of Sheffield started bus operations in the later years of the 1980s. No standard livery was maintained, as must vehicles were covered in adverts as exemplified by TCD 486J. This ex-Southdown Bristol RESL6L with Marshall bodywork was photographed over the road from Pond Street bus station in Sheffield on a damp summer's day in 1987.

Halifax Joint Committee was an independent bus company, despite taking the name and livery from the long-gone municipal operator absorbed by West Yorkshire PTE. The 'new' company started operations running a heritage service to Hebden Bridge, employing an AEC Regent III. Using former London Transport AEC Routemasters, Halifax Joint Committee expanded into commercial operations. One of them, WLT 324 (RM324 in London days), is seen amidst the Christmas lights in Halifax town centre in December 1997. (Jim Sambrooks)

Halifax Joint Committee, in later years, also ran a fleet of more conventional buses. One of them, registered H839 PVW, was photographed leaving Halifax bus station on 7 April 2010. This Alexander-bodied Leyland Olympian had started life as No. RH83 (91 D 1083) in the Dublin Bus fleet. Halifax Joint Committee ceased operations in 2014.

Holling's, based at the small South Yorkshire mining town of Askern, once ran a service from the rural village of Fenwick to Doncaster. Here, the bus used to lay over in the Waterdale coach park and, on 17 February 1962, it was photographed there by the Late Geoff Warnes. WJU 406, the regular performer, was a Leyland Leopard L2 that had originally been a demonstrator for bodybuilder Willowbrook.

The small East Yorkshire village of Newport was once home to Holts Coaches with a regular stage carriage run into nearby Goole. At the depot in 1978 is 414 FOR, a fifty-three-seat Leyland Leopard/Willowbrook bus that had been new to Winchester independent King Alfred.

Derbyshire operator Hulley's of Baslow have a regular service into the South Yorkshire city of Sheffield and that is where we see No. 14 (Q364 FVT) passing the railway station in the summer of 1996. The chassis of this bus, a Leyland Leopard, had started life in 1985, but had been given a fifty-two-seat Willowbrook Warrior body in 1992.

Good News Travel (Hunter) of Hull used the name Humber Stagecoach for its post-deregulation bus services in the city. Operating such a duty on Prospect Street in spring 1990 is Leyland National OKJ 514M, which had started life as Maidstone & District 3514 in 1974. Humber Stagecoach services are no longer being operated.

The Ideal Bus Service was a joint operation by Taylor's and H. Wray & Son. It is at the latter's yard in Cudworth that we see HJN 841 on the left, a former Southend Corporation Leyland PD2/20 with 'lowbridge' Weymann bodywork. Alongside is CCK 386, an ex-Ribble Leyland PD2/3, while behind is KHE 526. This had been new to Wray's as a 1947-built Leyland PS1/1 coach that had later received a Roe double-deck body. Ideal, operating in the area between Barnsley and Pontefract, lasted into the mid-1970s. The photograph was taken on 7 May 1967 by the late Les Flint.

The sparsely populated area to the south-east of Doncaster was once Lincolnshire Road Car territory, but has since been ceded to the local independent Isle Coaches. Based at the village of Owston Ferry, today's services provide road transport from the rural Lincolnshire villages into Scunthorpe and Doncaster. Seen in the latter town on 1 December 2012 is P927 RYO. This Northern Counties-bodied Volvo Olympian had started life with London General as a two-doored vehicle.

Following deregulation, Ivy Coaches commenced operations in the area around Dewsbury. Seen on that town's ring road, passing the John F. Kennedy public house in March 1989, is OEX 799W. This Willowbrook-bodied Leyland Leopard coach had been new to Eastern Counties as fleet number LL799. Ivy Coaches only lasted a few years in the stage carriage market.

Jaronda Travel once ran a service from Selby to Drax but expanded when it took over the former Majestic operations between Selby and York. Seen on such a duty in March 1991, arriving at its southerly destination, is H878 LOX. This thirty-nine-seat Duple-bodied Dennis Dart had been bought new by the company in 1990. Jaronda Travel later passed on the Arriva Group.

Kettlewells of Retford is a Nottinghamshire operator that once ran into Doncaster, in South Yorkshire. Photographed as it departed from that town's Southern bus station in early 1987 is GHV 67N. This Park Royal-bodied Daimler Fleetline had been new as a dual-doored bus with London Transport, where it had carried the number DM1067. Kettlewells are still in business, but no longer undertake stage carriage work.

K-Line began commercial bus operation in the Huddersfield area in 1986, following deregulation. Several Leyland Nationals were owned, including NWN 719M, a former South Wales Transport example. It was photographed in Huddersfield bus station in the spring of 1989. K-Line sold out to the Pride of the Road Group in 1993 and eventually ended up in the Centrebus empire.

Kirkby Lonsdale Coach Hire has expanded into the provision of bus services in the area north of Skipton, especially after the demise of Pennine Motor Services. One of the company's Optare Solo saloons, MX56 NLM, was found outside the village of Giggleswick on 21 November 2013. Note the incorrect 'Bristol' emblem on the front of the bus, a common practice by the company. This vehicle had come from another Yorkshire operator – Stringer's of Pontefract.

Another vehicle of Kirkby Lonsdale Coach Hire, PO62 LKF, is seen in the centre of Skipton on a dull 17 May 2017. This thirty-three-seat Wright Streetlite WF had been new to a Lancashire operator from Carnforth.

Ladyline (C Goodridge) was a coach business based near Rotherham. During early 1992 the company was operating service 293 to Dronfield (Derbyshire) via Sheffield, where we see ex-East Kent Leyland National JJG 901P. The company has since ceased trading.

Today the small town of Barnoldswick is in the grasps of Lancashire, but was within the boundaries of the West Riding of Yorkshire until 1974. It saw the birth of one of Britain's earliest bus companies, Ezra Laycock. Mr Laycock himself was from Cowling, a nearby village. Over the years, several services were developed, including the route into Skipton. At the depot in June 1970 we have a trio of ex-Ribble Leyland Titans (BCK 452, ECK 927 and BCK 437) plus an ex-City of Oxford AEC Regent V registered 968 CWL). Two years later, the business was sold to Pennine Motor Services. (Les Flint)

Samuel Ledgard Ltd entered the road passenger transport business in 1912, building up a sizeable route mileage that spread into both Leeds and Bradford, with one service even reaching Harrogate. Perhaps the best place to find the company's buses was the small town of Otley, where HGF 908 was photographed in the early 1960s. This Park Royal-bodied Daimler CWA6D had been new to London Transport in 1946, numbered as D231. Prior to entering service with Ledgards, it had been fitted with platform doors.

Also seen in Otley's bus station is GHN 631, a former United Automobile Bristol K6A/ECW of 1946 vintage. This 'lowbridge' vehicle was purchased for the Otley to Horsforth service, which passed under a height-restricted structure en route. Samuel Ledgard Ltd sold out to West Yorkshire Road Car Co. in 1967.

Leon Motor Services began stage carriage services in the 1920s, their main route being the one from their home village of Finningley into Doncaster. There were also occasional forays into Misson and Wroot. Over the years the company has had a great variety of vehicles and No. 49 (EF 7939) has been chosen to represent the early 1960s. This 1947-built Daimler CWD6 with centre-entrance Roe body had been new to West Hartlepool Corporation. It was photographed in the sun outside the depot.

Not all of the Leon Motor Services fleet was second-hand, as many new vehicles were purchased. Whether this one was bought new is a matter of conjecture. The chassis of No. 57 (432 KAL) had been built by Daimler as that company's first 30-foot-long (a CVD650/30) and was exhibited at the 1956 Commercial Vehicle Show. Daimler released the chassis in 1961 and it was fitted with a Roe seventy-three-seat body. As such, it was photographed leaving its Doncaster terminus in 1977. Leon Motor Services sold out to Mass Transit/BrightBus in 2004.

Leven Valley was in business for nearly thirty years, serving the South Teesside area. At least one of its routes ran into the North York Moors National Park. That is where we see Optare Solo MX05 OSW, passing the isolated Lion Inn, Blakey Ridge, on 31 July 2006. The twenty-four-seat bus had been new to Stanley Travel in County Durham.

In more urban surroundings, Leven Valley's T13 GAJ, named *St Bede*, was photographed in Middlesbrough town centre on 10 April 2010. This twenty-nine-seat Alexander Dennis Enviro 200 had been new in the previous year. Leven Valley was saved from closure in 2013 by Compass Royston Travel but ceased trading in 2015.

Longstaff's Coaches was founded in 1925 and the company was run by three generations of the Longstaff family. The service between Dewsbury and Mirfield has long been the mainstay of bus operations. At the depot, in the outskirts of Mirfield in spring 1980, we see YHD 599V. Bought new late in 1979, this is a relatively unusual Volvo B58-56 with sixty-three-seat Duple Dominant bus bodywork.

Longstaff's VCX 340X was also delivered new to the company in 1982. A Leyland Atlantean AN68C/2R with Northern Counties bodywork, this eighty-three-seat bus was photographed at its Mirfield terminus in the autumn of 1983. In 2011, the company was taken over by A. Lyles & Son, but the Longstaff name and blue livery was retained for the Dewsbury–Mirfield run.

Not to be confused with the operator mentioned on the previous page (though they were related), Ron Lyles & Son was a Batley operator that entered the stage carriage market after deregulation. A variety of second-hand saloons was owned, including XLJ 724K – a former Hants & Dorset Bristol RELL6G with dual-purpose ECW bodywork. It is seen in weak winter sunlight at Dewsbury bus station in December 1986. The Ron Lyles business went into receivership in September 2008.

M Travel, based at Glasshoughton, ran services in the Pontefract and Castleford areas of West Yorkshire. A variety of used double-deck buses was used on such duties. One of them, LG02 FCJ was found in central Castleford on 27 February 2015. It had been new to London United as a dual-door-fitted Dennis Trident/Alexander. M Travel lost its licence to operate in 2017.

M&T (Muffit & Taylor) Coaches was one of those short-lived independents that started operations in Leeds just after deregulation. One of their buses, TVF 705G, was photographed in central Leeds in early 1988, operating route 49 to Morley. This vehicle had been new to Eastern Counties as No. RL705, a Bristol RELL6G-bodied by ECW.

Burley's, trading as Majestic, once ran a stage carriage service between York and Selby via the company's home village of Cawood. Seen in Selby in 1981 is OWX 396K, a Bedford YRQ with Willowbrook forty-five-seat dual-purpose bodywork, bought new in 1972. The Majestic service later passed to Jaronda Travel and, later, into the hands of Arriva.

Leon Motor Services (see page 38) sold out to Mass Transit in 2004, which kept the bus services running for a few years. Operating a Doncaster to Hexthorpe duty in July 2006 was N598 DWY, a Dennis Dart/Plaxton that had been new to a Swansea operator. Mass Transit later became known as BrightBus, with the former Leon routes passing to First South Yorkshire. BrightBus ceased trading in 2017.

The River Maun flows through the Nottinghamshire town of Mansfield and that was the location of the HQ of Maun Coaches. This company ran several stage carriage services into South Yorkshire, including the historic small town of Tickhill, where E721 BVO was photographed in early 1988. This vehicle, a Mercedes 811D/Optare StarRider thirty-three-seat midibus, had been newly purchased in late 1987. The company's stage operations passed to Stagecoach East Midland in the early 1990s.

One of several independents to take advantage of deregulation in the city of Hull was Metro City Bus. In the summer of 1990, ex-East Kent Leyland National EFN 174L was photographed near Ferensway bus station on a local service to Bransholme. Metro City Bus later succumbed to the might of East Yorkshire Motor Services.

Another short-lived incumbent was Metropolitan Coaches, based at Monk Bretton and running into Barnsley. That is where we see FIL 7657 in late 1995. Originally registered SBA 637R when it was new to Stott of Oldham, it is a Plaxton-bodied Leyland Leopard. (Jim Sambrooks)

Miramare was a small company that tried competing on the lucrative Leeds to Morley service. Not all the company's vehicles received fleet livery, but NOE 591R certainly did and was photographed in Morley in mid-1991. This 1977-built Leyland National had been new as No. 591 in the Midland Red fleet.

Over the years, many small coach operators have operated market day stage carriage services into various Yorkshire towns. One such is Murgatroyd's of Pateley Bridge who, even today, take shoppers into Ripon. A fascinating variety of vehicles has been used since the 1950s, including Bedford OB types. In September 2013, RJI 8712 was employed on such a duty. This Volvo/ Jonckheere coach had originally been with Clyde Coast of Ayrshire. (Keith Jenkinson)

North Bank Travel was a Hull operator that took the opportunity to get into stage carriage work when Pride of the Road ceased their East Yorkshire operations. Seen in central Hull in spring 1998 is OOX 821R, a former West Midlands PTE Leyland National.

AUP 368W had started life with Northern General in 1980 as No. 3468. This Leyland Atlantean AN68B/1R with Roe bodywork was photographed in Hull with North Bank Travel in September 2000. Later, North Bank Travel became part of Applebys and the services soon passed on to Alpha.

Northern Bus 'morphed' out of the firm of A&C Wigmore of Dinnington, expanding in those years after deregulation in 1986. The company found a liking for the Bristol RE type, but an exception was No. 1231 (RHL 112X), seen outside Pond Street bus station in Sheffield in spring 1993, heading for Penistone. This vehicle had started life registered RDL 308X, with Southern Vectis, as an ECW-bodied Leyland Leopard.

Northern Bus No. 2478 (TCH 278L) was photographed on a sunny day in May 1993 at Sheffield's modernised bus station. This bus, a Bristol RELH6L with ECW bodywork, originally with dual-purpose seating, had been new to Midland General. Northern Bus later succumbed to the might of the area's larger operators.

Optional Bus was a smart, but short-lived, operator in Leeds. Double-deck vehicles were used, but a smaller vehicle has been chosen to represent the fleet. MCW Metrorider F186 YDA, ex-London Buses, is seen in Duncan Street, Leeds, in May 1999.

Paul's Travel, also trading as Fair Rider, ran a few bus services in Huddersfield in the early years of the twenty-first century. Plaxton-bodied Dennis Darts were employed, exemplified by K823 NKH, a former London Buses thirty-four-seat vehicle. It was photographed arriving at the town's bus station, *c.* 2005.

One of Yorkshire's best-known and loved independents, Pennine Motor Services, ceased trading in 2014. The original core route was from Skipton to Lancaster, via the company's main depot at Gargrave. Back in July 1962, Roe-bodied Leyland Royal Tiger NWT 807 is ready to depart from Skipton's bus station on a run through to Ingleton. Behind a Ribble Leyland Atlantean waits for passengers on an express service to Manchester, as a West Yorkshire Road Car Bristol LS saloon arrives. (Les Flint)

A former West Yorkshire Road Car Leyland National 2, originally registered PWY 583W, seen here as JIL 8353 with Pennine Motor Services, awaits its next duty in Skipton bus station in the summer of 2002. One of several Leyland Nationals in the fleet, these were later replaced by low-floor Dennis Darts.

Larratt Pepper (LP Coaches) of Thurnscoe became the last of the 'traditional' independents serving Barnsley. Latterly the company had a preference for Leyland Leopard saloons and coaches, but an exception was HWU 939J, a Plaxton-bodied Bedford YRQ. It was photographed close to the depot in 1978.

Sometime around 1977, Pepper's KHE 878P is seen leaving Barnsley bus station on a journey to Thurnscoe via Darfield. This Leyland Leopard with Duple Dominant coachwork had fifty-three seats and folding doors for stage carriage work. 1978 was the year that Yorkshire Traction took over the bus service, though the company continued with private hire, etc.

Powells was once a contract operator running buses for school transport in the Rotherham area. Originally based at Wickersley, the depot is now at Hellaby. In recent years the company has expanded into stage carriage work, serving Rotherham, Doncaster and Sheffield. On a local service on Eccleshall Road, Sheffield, we see OJD 835Y on 27 July 2006. This MCW Metrobus had originally been No. MB35 in the London Buses fleet.

Seen leaving Doncaster Interchange on 19 June 2013 is P814 YCW, owned by Powells. New in 1997, this Dennis Dart SLF/Wright saloon had started life with C&M of Aintree. In July 2018 Powells Bus was taken over by the HCT Group, a social enterprise operator.

Premier (Harold Wilson) of Stainforth participated for many years in the frequent Doncaster to Thorne Moorends operation, along with the other independents. Like Blue Line and Reliance, the company had a liking for Guy Arabs, three of which can be seen in this line up at the depot yard in 1974. In the centre are TWX 864 and YWX 644, both Roe-bodied Mark IV types, while an earlier Guy Arab is on the right, being cannibalised for spares. On the left is HYG 123C, a Daimler Fleetline, again bodied by Roe. (Les Flint)

Not all of Premier's service buses were double-deckers. Operating a Doncaster to Moorends service in 1982 is OWG 368X, a Plaxton-bodied Leyland Leopard capable of seating sixty-four passengers. It was photographed close to the Green Tree pub, just outside Hatfield Woodhouse. Premier lasted as an independent until June 1988, when South Yorkshire Transport took over.

Pride of the Dales was a minibus operator running a few rural services in the Skipton area. Seen in that town's bus station in late 1994 is VIA 179. The history of this Freight Rover Sherpa has proved elusive, but the 'cherished' registration was later transferred to the Optare Solo seen below.

This is Ilkley's small bus station on 6 September 2012, as Pride of the Dales' twenty-six-seat Optare Solo VIA 179 loads up for a run to Grassington. Pride of the Dales ceased trading in 2018 after the retirement of the owner.

Pride of the Road began services in the Barnsley area after deregulation. Departing from that town's bus station in the summer of 1990 is GHB 222W, a former Merthyr Tydfil Leyland National 2.

Pride of the Road also tried stage carriage work in the city of Hull. In mid-1994, beside Paragon railway station, the competition is overtaking Leyland National ORP 475M. This had started life as a fifty-two-seat bus with United Counties. Pride of the Road's East Yorkshire adventures did not last long and the Barnsley-based operations were sold to the Yorkshire Traction Group in 1992.

Primrose Valley Coaches once ran a service from the village of the same name into the nearby seaside town of Filey. A regular performer on this duty was RBT 637M, a fifty-five-seat Bedford YRT/Willowbrook saloon bought new in 1974. It was photographed at the depot in 1979. The service was later taken over by East Yorkshire Motor Services.

Rainworth Travel was another operator that entered the stage carriage market just after deregulation, mainly on tendered services. Though based over the border, some of the routes entered Yorkshire and it is in the mining community of New Rossington that we see FBX 562W in late 1986. This Bedford YMQ/Duple saloon had come from Welsh operator Davies of Pencader. The Rainworth Travel business was later taken over by Stagecoach East Midland.

Since 1949, Reliance of Stainforth (R Store) was a subsidiary of Blue Line, as previously illustrated on page 14. It was, however, retained as a separate unit and a lighter blue colour scheme was generally employed. It is seen applied to JWX 261, a 1950-built Leyland Comet with thirty-three-seat Barnaby bodywork. This fine vehicle was photographed in August 1962 at its terminus beside Christchurch in Doncaster. (Les Flint)

At Reliance's main depot, in Stainforth, we see one of many double-deck Guys in the fleet, photographed on 27 March 1963. MNU 777 had been new to a Derbyshire operator and was a Guy Arab III with Northern Coachbuilders bodywork. Like Blue Line, Reliance was bought by South Yorkshire PTE in 1979. (Les Flint)

The other company in Yorkshire called Reliance is the one that still operates in the area north of York to this day. The present owners bought the business in 1980, though bus operations started in 1930. On a freezing winter day in 1981, BVY 689R was photographed at its York terminus operating the original route to Brandsby. This Bedford YMT/Willowbrook saloon had been bought new for this duty.

Today, Reliance's main routes are between York and Easingwold. Sometime around 2005, beside Easingwold's Market Place, we see X618 VWR, a Wright-bodied Volvo B10BLE bought new in 2001. It is wearing the operator's current green livery.

During the late 1980s Revill Bus operated station carriage services in East Yorkshire. Seen at Beverley's bus station in March 1989 is NEV 688M, an ex-Eastern National Leyland National of 1974 vintage.

The original York Pullman is illustrated later on in these pages but was sold to Reynard Coaches in 1985. Deregulation saw bus services expand under the Reynard Pullman name. Bearing such a title, plus 'Yorbus' branding, is F363 BUA, a twenty-four-seat Dodge S56 with bodywork by Northern Counties. Reynard was sold to Yorkshire Rider in 1990.

A coach firm based in Hull, Rhodes began stage carriage operations in the city after deregulation. A small collection of second-hand vehicles was purchased, one of which, UNA 844S, was captured on film turning into Carr Lane in the city centre in early 1992. This Park Royal-bodied Leyland Atlantean AN68A/1R had been new as No. 7844 in the Greater Manchester PTE fleet.

Leyland National LPR 936P had started life as a forty-nine-seat vehicle with Hants & Dorset. Here it is seen with Rhodes of Hull, sitting in Ferensway bus station in mid-1992. Later that year the services were sold to East Yorkshire Motor Services.

Another firm named Rhodes entered into bus service provision after deregulation. This one was based in the small West Yorkshire town of Yeadon. Though the main route was on the Leeds to Otley corridor, other work was undertaken and here we see A6 RLR in central Leeds, heading for Whinmoor in early 1994. This bus had originally been a Van Hool A600 demonstrator registered G680 TKE.

Another unusual bus in the Rhodes of Yeadon fleet. The chassis of UOI 4323 had begun life as a Volvo B10M with a Van Hool coach body registered BKH 129X. It passed to Rhodes in 1987 and was rebodied by East Lancs in 1993. Here it is seen at the Central bus station in Leeds in late 1994, the year that Rhodes sold out to Yorkshire Rider.

Roger Richardson began his Sheffield-based coach business in 1976 and was able to enter the stage carriage market after deregulation. One of the company's coaches, FBU 302K, was photographed on service in 1986, a mile or so to the north of Chapeltown, having just passed over the M1. This AEC Reliance/Plaxton combination had been new to Mayne's of Manchester in 1972.

Here is another vehicle from the Manchester area that had found its way into the Richardson's fleet. JDK 924P had been new to Lancashire United of Atherton in 1975. This Plaxton-bodied Leyland Leopard service bus was photographed in Sheffield in the late 1980s. Roger Richardson later moved his business to Midhurst, West Sussex, where he died in 2011. His widow took over the business, but it ceased trading in 2019.

Ross Travel was established in 1968 in the former mining community of Featherstone, West Yorkshire. Like many other companies, stage carriage operations began following deregulation. These are run under the brand name of 'The Featherstone Rover'. An unusual vehicle for such duties, photographed in Pontefract in mid-1993, was HSC 169X. New to Lothian Buses in 1981, it is a Leyland Cub bodied by Duple to its 'Dominant' design.

Today most of the Ross Travel routes are the domain of the Optare Solo, one of which, YJ05 WCR, was photographed passing Castleford bus station on 27 February 2015. The company had purchased this thirty-three-seat vehicle new in 2005.

Rossie Motors, with a share of the Doncaster–Rossington service, started out in 1923. Perhaps one of its most interesting buses was DT 3692. The Daimler CP6 chassis of this vehicle had been new to Doncaster Corporation in 1932, but Rossie Motors had rebodied it in 1946 when it received a second-hand English Electric forty-eight-seat body. This had been donated by an ex-Hull Leyland TD2. In its rebuilt state, it is seen at Waterdale in Doncaster in the early 1950s.

Here is one of the more modern vehicles in the Rossie Motors fleet: RYG 545L, a Roe-bodied Daimler Fleetline bought new. It is seen departing from the South bus station in Doncaster in 1980, the year that South Yorkshire PTE took over.

Rotherham & District was set up by Glynn Pegg in 1989 to run services in South Yorkshire. Various vehicles were hired from other operators. At least one former London AEC Routemaster was used, but very few buses were painted into the fleet livery. One exception was ex-Midland Red Leyland National HHA 155L, photographed at Sheffield's Pond Street bus station in June 1990. Rotherham & District's bus services did not last much longer.

Another short-lived bus service provider was Roy's of Morley, West Yorkshire. Seen on service in the summer of 1988 is HUH 409N. This Leyland National had been new to Taff-Ely District Council, Pontypridd.

One of the few pre-deregulation independent operators in the north-east of Yorkshire was Saltburn Motor Services. A fleet of mainly lightweight vehicles was employed, an example being OAJ 901. This Bedford SBO with forty-seat Duple Midland bodywork, bought new in 1956, was photographed in Saltburn on 16 April 1963. In 1974 Cleveland Transit purchased the fleet and operations. (Peter Tuffrey Collection)

Selwyn Motors ran a Saturday service from its home village of Belton in Lincolnshire to Doncaster, giving passengers a few hours to do their shopping, etc. The bus used to lie over beside Christchurch, where OJD 138R was photographed in spring 1986. This Leyland Fleetline/Park Royal had started life as DMS2138 in the London Buses fleet. The service ceased in early 2017.

Another Doncaster area independent that used Christchurch as a terminal was T. Severn & Sons of Dunscroft. From 1922 the company had operated a share of the busy Doncaster to Thorne route and also to the nearby villages. Virtually all service buses since the 1960s were bought new, including 819 CWW, seen here at Christchurch *c.* 1977. It is a Leyland PD3/4 with a seventy-two-seat Roe body.

Severn's SWR 4L was photographed outside the substantial depot in Dunscroft in the mid-1970s. This Leyland Atlantean AN68/1R carried a Roe body, with seventy-two seats. In 1979 the business of T. Severn & Sons was purchased by South Yorkshire PTE. (Jim Sambrooks)

Shaun's Minibus & Coach Hire ran a few rural services in North Yorkshire. Seen in Ripon on 21 February 2016 is LK58 CUA, an Optare Tempo saloon using hybrid technology. It had been new to Metroline in London. Sadly, operations ceased when the company's owner died in 2017. (Jim Sambrooks)

Sheaf Line was set up to operate bus services around Sheffield in the years after deregulation. Double-deck vehicles were employed including WWH 44L, a Daimler Fleetline/Park Royal vehicle that had been new to SELNEC in 1973. It was photographed in Fitzalan Square, Sheffield, in autumn 1988. Sheaf Line was purchased by South Yorkshire PTE in 1990.

Sheffield Omnibus commenced operations in 1991. Pressed into service without being fully repainted in 1993 was OYJ 65R. This East Lancs-bodied Leyland Atlantean AN68/1R had been new to Brighton Buses and was still partly wearing that livery when photographed outside Pond Street bus station. Sheffield Omnibus sold out to the Yorkshire Traction Group in 1995.

Shoreline Suncruisers began operating open-top buses on Scarborough's seafront in 1991. These operations continue today, but the company now has some 'normal' stage carriage workings too. Covered top double-deck buses are used on these, one of which would have been YBK 337V. When photographed on the Promenade in July 2005 this bus was operating a schools duty. It had been new in 1979 as an Alexander-bodied Leyland Atlantean AN68/1R to Portsmouth City Transport. Low-floor buses operate present-day bus services.

Silver Star once ran a service from Carleton into Skipton. A regular performer on such a duty was GOU 721, a Duple-bodied Bedford OB built in 1949. It had originated with a Horsham operator. Here it is, crossing the railway near Skipton loco shed, *c.* 1960, before Silver Star sold out to Ezra Laycock in 1961.

In the years after deregulation, Silverwing of Hull entered into stage carriage work. On such a duty, ready for a journey to Hedon, TUG 811R was photographed in central Hull in spring 1990. This Leyland National had originally been No. 27 in the Yorkshire Woollen District fleet.

In the summer of 1987 Skill's of Nottingham were operating a few tendered stage carriage services in South Yorkshire. One of them was route N19, in the hands of twenty-three-seat MCW Metrorider D72 WTO. It was photographed at the stop serving the Falcon pub in Dinnington heading for 'Darnell', a misspelling of Darnall. Skill's are still in business today, but no longer undertake service bus work.

South Riding was yet another operator competing in Sheffield. In 1994 one of several Leyland Nationals in the fleet was found in the city centre. No. 39 (SWE 446S) had come from Yorkshire Traction and would soon go back there upon the takeover in the same year.

South Yorkshire Road Transport (SYRT) was, in fact, from what is now West Yorkshire! The firm was based in a depot in Pontefract and ran a Leeds to Doncaster service, as well as routes towards Barnsley and, on certain days, Selby. In the post-war years the company had a preference for Albions, such as 61 (GWT 630). This Burlingham-bodied Albion Valkyrie CX13 had been bought new in 1947. It was photographed in the centre of Pontefract, *c.* 1960, and has since been preserved.

Another Albion in the SYRT fleet, No. 81 (TWY 8), seen in Pontefract in the mid-1960s. This vehicle had started life as a Burlingham-bodied coach but had been given a new Roe body in 1958. It has also entered preservation. (Les Flint)

In the latest livery of the time, *c.* 1975, SYRT 83 (2600 WW) was photographed in Pontefract town centre. This Leyland PD3/1 was fitted with a 'lowbridge' Roe body, capable of seating sixty-seven passengers.

SYRT's last livery is shown to good effect in Pontefract bus station on a sunny day in spring 1988. The vehicle, No. 92 (NWX 992M), is a Daimler Fleetline with seventy-seat Northern Counties bodywork. South Yorkshire Road Transport sold out to the Caldaire Group, owners of West Riding Automobile Company, in 1994.

SquarePeg is a newcomer to the West Yorkshire bus scene. Though it mainly provides school buses, the company also runs a few stage carriage services. The most frequent of these is route 9, which serves Seacroft bus station. On 4 December 2019, Y173 HRN was photographed here. It is a Wright-bodied Volvo B10BLE that had been new to Transdev Lancashire United.

Stagecarriage is another company that has recently appeared, this time on the roads around Middlesbrough. Seen in that town's bus station is YN03 DFC, an East Lancs-bodied Scania N94UD. Photographed on 25 April 2018, it had been new to Metrobus in Surrey.

Star Travel of Wakefield has had the occasional dabble with bus service provision. In spring 1988 it was using NUD 77M on its route into Wakefield. Originally a dual-purpose ECW-bodied Bristol RELH6L, it had been new to City of Oxford Motor Services.

Station Coaches, though based in Batley, provide a frequent service between Ossett and Wakefield. Seen passing through that city's Bull Ring on 5 May 2016 is Y48 HHE. This Wright-bodied Scania L94UB had been new as a Heathrow car park shuttle vehicle.

Stephensons of Easingwold once ran several stage carriage services into the city of York. Seen here on a wet day in autumn 2003, beside the railway station, is S309 KNW. This DAF SB220 with Optare 'Delta' bodywork had been new as an Optare demonstrator. In early 2018, Stephensons ceased operating and the services passed to York Pullman.

Steve Stockdale Coaches once provided town services in both Selby and Goole. Sometime around 1986, serving the latter location, we see FSA 191V. It is an ex-Northern Scottish Ford R1014 with Alexander Y type bodywork. The company was rather short-lived in the world of stage carriage work.

Stotts Coaches of Milnsbridge, Huddersfield, (not to be confused with the Oldham firm with the same name) run several services around the company's home town. Typical of the fleet, Optare Solo YK05 CCN, ex-Metroline of London, was photographed in Slaithwaite on 16 May 2014.

Another Huddersfield independent, Streamline, started operations in 2012. Low-floor Dennis Dart/Plaxton vehicles are the norm on the bus routes, including V166 MVX, photographed in the town centre on 3 April 2014. This bus had started life with East London Buses.

Stringers of Pontefract started coaching operations in 1953 but has only been running stage carriage services in relatively recent years. Today's routes serve Pontefract and Castleford and it is in the latter town, on 27 February 2015, that we see MB04 BLF. Originally registered J5 BUS with Jim Stones of Leigh, it is a Transbus Dart SLF with Transbus (Plaxton) 'Pointer' bodywork.

Swifts Travel was a short-lived entrant into the stage carriage world of Doncaster. In early 1994, YEL 92Y is about to enter the town's South bus station. This coach is an ex-Hants & Dorset Leyland Leopard with ECW bodywork. (Jim Sambrooks)

Tate's Travel was founded in 2003 and, two years later, began running bus services in Barnsley. On 18 August 2010 the company was using R467 LGH on service, when it was photographed close to the town's Interchange. The vehicle, a Dennis Dart SLF/Plaxton saloon, had been new to London Central.

Tate's Travel later expanded into West Yorkshire, including Dewsbury, where ex-Goodwin's of Manchester Wright StreetLite WF MX60 GWO was photographed on 24 April 2014. Just under two years later the company went into administration.

Taylor's Coaches were running stage carriage services in Leeds during the 1990s, notably on the Leeds–Morley corridor. On such duties, passing the city's famous Markets on a wet autumn day in 1990, is NHL 561M. This Leyland National had been new to West Riding as fleet No. 361.

Like another Leeds independent of the time, Taylor's Coaches operated at least one Volvo Ailsa. JOV 741P had been one of several B55-10 types bodied by Alexander in the West Midlands PTE fleet. It is seen on Vicar Lane in central Leeds in November 1993. Christmas is coming!

Thompson Travel's vehicles were to be seen on Sheffield's streets during the 1990s. Operating a bus service there in late 1994 was YFC 14R, an ex-City of Oxford Leyland Leopard/Duple Dominant coach. The company also owned a Leyland Lynx at one time.

2019 saw the seventieth anniversary of the founding of the business of JH Thornes Coach Proprietor and Motor Engineer. The firm has long operated some stage carriage work, mainly into the market town of Selby. At the depot in 1978 is a unique vehicle, registered MBO 1F. This had come from Western Welsh, who had fitted a 1961 Weymann body from an Albion Nimbus to a 1968 Bristol LHS6L chassis.

Arriving at Selby's main bus terminal, in the shadow of the abbey and beside the railway station in March 1991, is Thornes' XKU 229T. This Bedford YMT/Willowbrook saloon had been new to the National Coal Board, where it was used for transporting miners and other workers.

Thornes, now based at Hemingbrough, still operates bus services today. The regular performer in the early twenty-first century was OKP 980, a Ford Transit minibus that had taken the registration of a former Maidstone and District Beadle-Leyland coach. It was photographed in Selby in summer 2001.

TLC Coaches was founded in 2000 and has since expanded considerably throughout West Yorkshire. Much of the fleet consists of Optare Solo saloons, such as this twenty-seater, No. 2609 (MX07 BCV). It was photographed at Ilkley bus station on 6 September 2012.

Seen in central Bradford on 14 November 2012 is TLC No. 12877 (MX12 DZG), an Alexander Dennis Enviro E20D twenty-eight-seat saloon, bought new.

County Durham operator Trimdon Motor Services expanded considerably after deregulation and even ventured into Yorkshire, albeit just over the border into Middlesbrough. At that town's bus station in spring 1988, we see a Leyland National 2 registered DMS 18V, which had previously served with Midland Scottish. Trimdon Motor Services later sold out to the Caldaire Group.

Another foreigner in Yorkshire! Tyrer Bus was a Lancashire operator, but it had a stage service into Skipton, where YJ51 EKP was photographed in the summer of 2002. This DAF SB200 with forty-four-seat Ikarus bodywork later passed with the service to the Transdev Group, but was soon sold to Irvine's of Law, Scotland.

United Services was the fleet name given to the joint bus service operations of the firms Everett's of South Kirkby, Bingley's of Kinsley and Cooper Bros of South Elmsall. Everett's ceased taking part in the 1960s, but Cooper Bros continued into the 1970s. At the Cooper Bros depot in South Kirkby on 7 May 1967, ex-Doncaster Corporation 'lowbridge' AEC Regent III/Roe 135 (MDT 220) was photographed. (Les Flint)

Cooper Bros were also the owners of ANF 161B. New to Manchester Corporation in 1964, it was a Park Royal-bodied Leyland Panther Cub. It was photographed at South Kirkby depot in 1977.

The other of the United Services constituents was WR&P Bingley. At their Upton depot we see LTO 10, *c.* 1960. This fine vehicle, a 'lowbridge' Daimler CVD6/Duple, had come from Skill's of Nottingham. The United Services business and the Doncaster–Wakefield route was sold to West Yorkshire PTE in 1977.

Universal Buses Limited was a Rochdale operator that could also be found in Yorkshire – just! The company had a route that served Todmorden, which is where we see R812 WJA in mid-1999. New to the company in 1997, it is a Dennis Dart SLF with UVG thirty-eight-seat bodywork. Universal Buses Limited was bought out by Stagecoach in 2000.

Wallace Arnold was once one of Britain's largest independent operators. Although most of its business was in the high-class coaching world, a small amount of stage carriage work was undertaken. In Leeds, these services were run under the names of 'Farsley Omnibus' and 'Kippax Motors'. Bearing the latter identification, Leyland PD3/1 6237 UB with Roe bodywork was photographed in Leeds Central bus station in March 1968. (Les Flint)

Wallace Arnold also ran a rural route out of Scarborough bearing the fleet name Hardwick's, mainly using Leyland Leopard coaches fitted with folding doors. Here is a night view, *c.* 1977, of such a vehicle, KUM 508L, bodied by Plaxton in Scarborough. Wallace Arnold's West Yorkshire operations were sold to Leeds Corporation in 1968, while the Scarborough routes went to East Yorkshire Motor Services in 1987. Wallace Arnold was later merged with Shearings.

TJ Walsh operates several routes in an around Halifax, mainly using minibuses. One of the largest vehicles owned, MX07 NTN, is seen in central Halifax on 27 March 2017. It is a Plaxton Primo saloon that had been originally delivered to a Birkenhead operator.

R&S Waterson's have been serving the Barnsley area since the 1980s and are still in business today. Modern buses tend to be in an all-white livery but, back in 1989, CNY 812V was bearing plenty of identification. This unusual Ford AO609/Moseley minibus had been new to South Wales operator Mainline of Tonyrefail. It was photographed in central Barnsley. (Jim Sambrooks)

Until its sale to the Transport Holding Company in 1967, the West Riding Automobile Company was Britain's largest independent bus company. On this page are a couple of photos taken prior to that date. Here we have No. 610 (AHL 122), a 1945-built Guy Arab II with 'lowbridge' Roe bodywork. It was photographed in Wakefield bus station, *c.* 1960.

Now we are Selby depot yard on 23 August 1962. Prominent on the left is the unique No. 751 (FHL 987), a Seddon Mark II with forty-four-seat Duple Midland bodywork. Keeping it company are rebuilt Leyland PS1/1 No. 790 (AHL 806) and AEC Reliance/Roe saloon 923 (THL 923). (Les Flint)

In the early 1990s a bus company called White Rose was running several bus services in West Yorkshire. It became well known for operating a fleet of ex-London AEC Routemaster, but also had some more conventional buses. One of them, NOC 727R, was photographed in Castleford in early 1992. This East Lancs-bodied Leyland Fleetline had been new as No. 6727 to West Midlands PTE.

Back in late 1986, Derbyshire operator Whites Tours of Calver were running the X65 service from Buxton to Sheffield. The city's Pond Street terminal was where VRB 899K was photographed. New to the company, it is a Bedford YRQ with Duple Viceroy Express forty-five-seat coachwork, ideal for such a journey.

A&C Wigmore, bus operators of Dinnington, could trace the company's history back to just after the First World War. For many years a service from Dinnington (a large South Yorkshire mining community) to Sheffield was operated. Photographed at Pond Street bus station in that city, in 1973, was SWY 334L, a Bedford YRT/Willowbrook saloon new to Wigmores in the previous year.

Wigmores later underwent a metamorphosis to become Northern Bus (see page 47) and, just before that event, F318 EWF was photographed in Dinnington in early 1989. The vehicle is a DAF SB220 with Optare Delta fifty-one-seat dual-purpose bodywork.

Wilfreda Coaches, from the Bawtry area around the South Yorkshire/Nottinghamshire border, was founded in 1949. In 1987 the company took over Beehive Services of Adwick-le-Street, just north of Doncaster. Hence the combined business was named Wilfreda Beehive. Deregulation saw the business expand into bus service work and a fleet of Leyland Nationals was acquired. One of these, ex-East Kent JJG 901P, was photographed in the South bus station in Doncaster in summer 1992.

Wilfreda Beehive later disposed of its bus routes, but has since re-entered the market, operating various services under tender from local councils. One such was the 'Airport Arrow' running from Doncaster to Robin Hood Airport, formerly known as RAF Finningley. For this duty Optare Tempo saloon YJ05 XOO was purchased, photographed on West Street, Doncaster, in the summer of 2005.

Woods of Mirfield had, for many years, been operating a Dewsbury–Mirfield route. In 1977 the regular performer on such duties was KTD 551C, a Leyland Atlantean PDR1/1-bodied by Park Royal. It had been new as a Leyland demonstrator and carried a plaque to state that it had been exhibited at a Commercial Motor Exhibition in Earls Court. This photograph was taken at the Dewsbury terminus, opposite the bus station.

In 1983 Woods of Mirfield was sold to Abbeyways, who maintained the services under its old identity. Bearing the Woods name at Dewsbury in mid-1986 is Q652 WWJ. This Leyland Leopard/Alexander saloon had been new as a Leyland demonstrator for Singapore in 1979. During its time there, it failed to attract any orders, so was returned to the UK in 1982. It later saw service with Allander of Milngavie in Scotland.

York Pullman was, undoubtedly, one of Britain's favourite independents. Founded in 1926, the company had routes out of York serving the areas to the north and east of the city. Seen in York awaiting departure for Stamford Bridge (scene of the lesser-known 1066 battle) is No. 87 (TDN 387H). This AEC Swift with a fifty-two-seat Roe body constructed on Park Royal frames was photographed in 1977.

York Pullman No. 109 (PDN 209M) is seen at its Exhibition Square stand in York city centre in 1981. Like most of the vehicles in this fleet, this Bedford YRT/Plaxton Elite Express coach had been bought new. In January 1985 the York Pullman business was sold to Reynard Coaches.

The York Pullman name did not die in 1985. A firm called K&J Logistics revived the livery and York Pullman was born again in 2007. Wearing the smart colours is No. 276 (NXI 4241), seen on a rail replacement duty at Leeds station on 21 July 2010. This Leyland Tiger with Alexander (Belfast) bodywork had been new to Ulsterbus in 1989.

One of York Pullman's newest vehicles is YX69 NUY, an Alexander Dennis Enviro E20D thirty-seat saloon. On a cold and wet 18 November 2019 this bus is seen close to Lendal Bridge in York, on route 21 from Colton.

Yorkshire Line Bus Company was a short-lived operator serving West Yorkshire. Seen in Wakefield on 10 February 2011 is P142 TDL, a UVG-bodied Dennis Dart. It had been new to the Isle of Wight County Council. Yorkshire Line ceased operations later in 2011.

Yorkshire Terrier began operations in Sheffield after deregulation. Second-hand Leyland Nationals were the first choice in the early days. Here is a former East Kent example, registered NFN 65M. It was photographed in central Sheffield in autumn 1988.

As an established operator, Yorkshire Terrier soon ordered new vehicles. One of these was No. 109 (K9 YTB), a Dennis Dart/Plaxton forty-seat saloon. It is seen at the Sandtoft trolleybus museum gathering, operating a car park duty, in July 1993. The Yorkshire Terrier business was purchased by Yorkshire Traction in 1995.

Yorkshire Travel was another independent that did not have a long life in the stage carriage market. One of the company's buses, SKF 14T, a former Merseyside PTE Leyland National, was found on Northgate, Wakefield, in March 1992. The company had been taken over by Caldaire by 1994.